S0-ADC-315

Daniel
in the
Lions' Den

Cover illustration by	Story adaptation by	Interior illustrations by
Randy Hamblin	Sarah Toast	Thomas Gianni

Interior art consultation by
David M. Howard, Jr., Ph.D.

Copyright © 1995 Publications International, Ltd.
All rights reserved. This book may not be reproduced or quoted in whole or in part by mimeograph or any other printed or electronic means, or for presentation on radio, television, videotape, or film without written permission from

Louis Weber, C.E.O.
Publications International, Ltd.
7373 North Cicero Avenue
Lincolnwood, Illinois 60646

Permission is never granted for commercial purposes.

Manufactured in U.S.A.

8 7 6 5 4 3 2 1

ISBN: 0-7853-2217-5

PUBLICATIONS INTERNATIONAL, LTD.
Rainbow is a trademark of Publications International, Ltd.

Long ago, King Nebuchadnezzar's army surrounded the city of Jerusalem. For nearly two years, the Babylonian army would not let anyone go in or out of Jerusalem.

When the people of Jerusalem had no food left, the army conquered the city. They took Hebrew captives and treasure from the temple back to Babylon.

Nebuchadnezzar's palace master picked out some of the smartest and handsomest young men from the noble Hebrew families to serve the king. One of these young men was Daniel.

Nebuchadnezzar treated the men well. Daniel was taught everything he needed to know to become the king's advisor.

Daniel was given good food and wine from the king's table, but he ate only the foods that were allowed by God. God was pleased with Daniel and gave him great wisdom and the special gift of understanding dreams.

Nebuchadnezzar also was pleased with Daniel's wisdom. Daniel lived in the palace for many years. He served Nebuchadnezzar and other kings that followed. One king was Belshazzar.

Belshazzar was a young king who did not know Daniel. One night Belshazzar invited his lords to a great dinner.

The king drank too much wine. Then he asked for the golden cups that Nebuchadnezzar had brought from the temple in Jerusalem many years before. The guests drank wine from the sacred cups and praised their gods.

Suddenly King Belshazzar stared at a strange hand that appeared to be writing a message of doom on the palace wall. Belshazzar's mother sent for Daniel to tell what the strange writing meant.

The words meant that Belshazzar had angered God and would soon lose his kingdom. That very night, the Persian soldiers entered Babylon. They killed Belshazzar and put Darius, their own king, on the throne.

Daniel became an important official. He did his job so well that Darius planned to let him run the kingdom.

This made the king's other officials jealous, and they set a trap for Daniel. They tricked Darius into signing a law that said the people could pray only to the king for one month.

Daniel heard about the king's law, but he followed God's law. Just as he had always done, Daniel went home three times every day to pray to God. He still looked out toward Jerusalem and kneeled in prayer.

The three jealous men told the king about Daniel's prayers to God. The king knew then that he had been tricked into harming Daniel. But the law was firm. King Darius had no other choice but to have Daniel thrown into a den of hungry lions as the punishment for breaking the new law.

The king was very upset. He tried until sundown to think of some way to save Daniel, but any law signed by the king could not be changed.

The unhappy king said to Daniel, "May your God, whom you faithfully serve, save you."

Then the king gave the command, and Daniel was thrown into the den of lions. A very heavy stone was laid over the mouth of the den so that there would be no way out. The king himself sealed the stone to make sure that no one could help Daniel escape.

King Darius went sadly back to his palace. He didn't even eat that evening. He was not able to sleep that night.

At daybreak, the king got up from his bed, and he hurried out to see the den of lions.

Darius called out, "O Daniel, faithful servant of God. Has your God saved you from the lions?"

Then from the den of lions Daniel's voice was heard. "O king, because I did no wrong, my God has sent his angel down to shut the lions' mouths so they would not hurt me."

This wonderful news made King Darius exceedingly happy. He commanded that Daniel be brought out of the lions' den immediately.

The heavy stone was moved away. And the men threw down ropes to haul Daniel out.

Everybody looked closely at Daniel. They were amazed to see that he had not been hurt at all by the lions. He had not even been scratched.

No kind of harm had come to Daniel in the lions' den because he had stayed faithful to God.

Then the king's thoughts turned to the men who had tried to have Daniel killed. Darius ordered some guards to bring the three men who had tricked him to appear at the palace.

The king had to decide the fate of the three men. The jealous plotters had planned for Daniel to be thrown into the lions' den, so the king decided that they should have the same punishment.

The three men were thrown down to the lions. But unlike when Daniel was in the den, no power stopped the hungry lions this time.

King Darius wrote to all the nations of the world, "I wish you all good things. In my kingdom, the people shall all worship the God of Daniel. The living God has saved him from the power of the lions!"

From that day on, Daniel lived in peace in King Darius's land.